For Mom and Dad,
who, as Fred Rogers said, loved me into being
—L. R.

To Dylan and Daniel
—B. B.

Selected Sources

"MISTER ROGERS' NEIGHBORHOOD | 1969 Senate Hearing | PBS Kids." YouTube. March 19, 2017.
youtube.com/watch?v=J9uIJ-o2yqQ&t=18s

"Mister Rogers' Neighborhood: A History." The Fred Rogers Company. nd. Accessed January 30, 2018.
fredrogers.org/fred-rogers/bio/index-test.php

"Mister Rogers' Neighborhood." PBS. nd. pbs.org/parents/rogers

"Mister Rogers' Neighborhood | By Topic." The Neighborhood Archive. nd. Accessed April 20, 2018.
neighborhoodarchive.com/mrn/episodes/index.html#topic

𝒜 atheneum ATHENEUM BOOKS FOR YOUNG READERS • An imprint of Simon & Schuster Children's Publishing Division • 1230 Avenue of the Americas, New York, New York 10020 • Text copyright © 2020 by Laura Renauld • Illustrations copyright © 2020 by Brigette Barrager • All rights reserved, including the right of reproduction in whole or in part in any form. • ATHENEUM BOOKS FOR YOUNG READERS is a registered trademark of Simon & Schuster, Inc. Atheneum logo is a trademark of Simon & Schuster, Inc. • For information about special discounts for bulk purchases, please contact Simon & Schuster Special Sales at 1-866-506-1949 or business@simonandschuster.com. • The Simon & Schuster Speakers Bureau can bring authors to your live event. For more information or to book an event, contact the Simon & Schuster Speakers Bureau at 1-866-248-3049 or visit our website at www.simonspeakers.com. • Book design by Lauren Rille • The text for this book was set in Bookman. • The illustrations for this book were rendered in gouache, colored pencil, and Photoshop. • Manufactured in China • 1019 SCP • First Edition • 10 9 8 7 6 5 4 3 2 1 • Library of Congress Cataloging-in-Publication Data • Names: Renauld, Laura, author. | Barrager, Brigette, illustrator. • Title: Fred's big feelings : the life and legacy of Mister Rogers / Laura Renauld ; illustrated by Brigette Barrager. • Description: First edition. | New York : Atheneum Books for Young Readers, an imprint of Simon & Schuster Children's Publishing Division, [2019] | Audience: Ages 4-8. | Audience: Grades K–3. • Identifiers: LCCN 2018043166 (print) | ISBN 9781534441224 (hardcover) | ISBN 9781534441231 (eBook) • Subjects: LCSH: Rogers, Fred—Juvenile literature. | Television personalities—United States—Biography— Juvenile literature. Classification: LCC PN1992.4.R56 R46 2019 (print) | DDC 791.4502/8092 [B]—dc23 • LC record available at https://lccn.loc.gov/2018043166

This book is not associated with or authorized by Fred Rogers Productions.

Fred's Big Feelings

The Life and Legacy of Mister Rogers

written by
Laura Renauld

illustrated by
Brigette Barrager

Atheneum Books for Young Readers
New York   London   Toronto   Sydney   New Delhi

Hello, neighbor!

It's a beautiful day. Come in.
Look around. What do you see?

This is the closet filled with Mister
Rogers' cardigans. His mother knitted
each one! And here's where he changes
his shoes. Sneakers are more comfy,
don't you think?

Now settle in. Mister Rogers is ready
to visit with you!

You may know Mister Rogers as
America's favorite television neighbor.
But before that . . .

. . . he was Freddy Rogers, a quiet boy with big feelings.

Freddy was shy, and he had trouble making friends. He felt *sad* when his schoolmates overlooked him.

Bullies taunted Freddy about his weight. He felt *scared* when they chased him home.

And when asthma kept him indoors for much of the summer, he felt *lonelier* than ever.

Freddy took refuge at the piano. Soon, his feelings were flowing through his fingertips.

Worry fretted and fussed . . . and faded.

Sadness wailed and whimpered . . . and waned.

Anger crashed and clattered . . . and calmed.

Music allowed Freddy to express himself, but it was his grandfather McFeely's message of unconditional love that boosted Freddy's self-esteem: "You made this day a really special day just by being yourself . . . and I happen to like you just the way you are."

Gradually, with Grandfather McFeely's words tucked
inside his heart, and music as his confidante, Fred grew.
In high school, when a football injury landed a popular player in
the hospital, Fred was there to bring Jim's homework to him.
A dynamic friendship developed between the two.

Jim accepted Fred. He vouched for him and encouraged him.

Fred's confidence soared. He became a leader. He felt *valued*
and *respected*.

How deeply one person can affect the life of another!

In the spring of 1951, Fred's path was clear: graduate from college, then attend seminary to become a minister.

But the new television set at his parents' house changed his plans. A children's show caught his attention. It left him feeling *shocked*.

To Fred, television had potential. What if he could create a thoughtful alternative to the endless pranks, jokes, and gags that filled the current programming? What if a TV show could leave someone feeling *welcomed*? *Loved?* Even . . . *special*? Fred was determined to find out.

His opportunity came at WQED, America's first community-supported television station. In 1954, Fred and his colleague Josie Carey created *The Children's Corner*. It was filled with Fred's music, Josie's laughter, and many puppets, which Fred animated from behind the scenes. His hunch that television could build a community while being entertaining *and* educational proved correct.

Their show was a hit!

The Children's Corner was performed live and mainly improvised. After it went off the air, Fred wanted to be more intentional about the content of his shows. So, in 1968, Fred started airing his own program: *Mister Rogers' Neighborhood*.

Now Fred was in front of the camera as the show's host. He welcomed children with his songs, encouraged his viewers' curiosity, and honored his grandfather by naming a character after him: Mr. McFeely, the Speedy Delivery man.

But above all, Fred focused on feelings: *silly*, *shy*, *selfish* . . . he addressed them all.

Look! Mister Rogers feels *playful*.
He is taking a juggling lesson.

Mister Rogers feels *sad*.
One of his goldfish has died.

Mister Rogers feels *welcoming*.
He invites Officer Clemmons
to soak his feet.

Mister Rogers feels *joyful*. He visits with special guests, like cellist Yo-Yo Ma, dancer Ying Li, jazz trumpeter Wynton Marsalis, and even Koko the Gorilla.

Now, listen! Here comes the trolley. . . .
Ding! Ding! Toot! Toot!

It's a world of make-believe!

The small tiger feels *worried*.

What if a falling star lands on his clock?

The king's niece feels *generous*.

She offers orange juice to each of her friends.

The rosy-cheeked lady feels *angry*.
She turns a tower upside down!
Toot! Toot! Ding! Ding! See you next time.

Grandfather McFeely knew Fred was one of a kind—and now America's children did too. All over the country, viewers were beginning to depend on his steady, caring presence.

But in 1969, when Fred's show was only one year old, the government threatened to cut the funding for public television. So Fred stepped off the set of *Mister Rogers' Neighborhood* and into a hearing on Capitol Hill to make his feelings known.

In front of a Senate committee, Fred testified about the important work of childhood: to learn how to express emotions constructively.

Even though Fred felt *mad*, he didn't shout or blame or raise his voice. Instead, he recited a song that he had written for his show called "What Do You Do with the Mad That You Feel?" In it, he encouraged children to draw on their inner strengths to communicate anger in healthy ways.

A hush fell over the room during Fred's quiet, passionate testimony. The tough committee chairman, Senator Pastore, even got goosebumps. "Looks like you just earned the twenty million dollars," he remarked.

By sharing his feelings, Fred Rogers secured the funding for public broadcasting. *Mister Rogers' Neighborhood* would be on the air for years to come.

In nearly nine hundred episodes, from 1968 to 2001,
Mister Rogers broadcasted *affection*, *compassion*,
and *respect* for his audience.

His message was clear:
It is normal to have feelings.
It is good to talk about feelings.
It is important to share feelings.
And the best part? Everyone expresses their feelings
in their own special way.

Our visit with Mister Rogers has come
to an end. It's time for him to feed the fish,
change out of his sneakers, and hang up
his sweater.

Now, listen! Mister Rogers has a message
just for you:

"You always make each day such a special day. You know how? Just by being you! There's only one person in the whole world like you, and people can like you exactly as you are."

That's such a good feeling!

Author's Note

Fred Rogers was once asked how the success of *Mister Rogers' Neighborhood* could be replicated. He replied, "I think that somehow you must remember what it was like to be a child." Fred Rogers did just that. He remembered his lonely childhood in Latrobe, Pennsylvania, a quiet suburb of Pittsburgh, during the 1930s. He remembered feeling things deeply, and adults brushing those feelings aside. He remembered how his piano and his puppets listened to him.

Fred started his television career working for NBC in New York City. With some experience under his belt, Fred moved back to Pittsburgh and into the realm of children's television. It was during his years on *The Children's Corner* at WQED that Fred began his habit of changing into sneakers. He needed to run quietly behind the scenes from one side of the set, where he played the organ, to the other, where he acted as puppeteer. This practical habit would later become the iconic beginning of *Mister Rogers' Neighborhood*.

Despite his busy schedule on *The Children's Corner*, Fred still found time during his lunch hour to attend seminary. In 1963, he was ordained as a Presbyterian minister. The church recognized the significance of Fred's work, so he was given a unique assignment: to continue working with children through the mass media.

Mister Rogers' Neighborhood grew out of a show Fred created for the Canadian Broadcasting Corporation in Toronto called *Misterogers*. It was there that he debuted in front of the camera as the show's host and developed his conversational style, connecting to children as a role model rather than as an entertainer. When Fred and his wife, Joanne, decided they wanted to raise their two young sons in the United States, they returned to Pittsburgh.

It was very important to Fred that the social and emotional themes he explored on his show were viewed through the lens of childhood. He took classes in developmental psychology and consulted with leading experts to bring the best practices in child development to *Mister Rogers' Neighborhood*. Every word in the show mattered to Fred. He didn't want his child viewers to misunderstand a phrase or feel confused. The writers had a word for the precise language Fred used: "Freddish."

And while *Mister Rogers' Neighborhood* was created for a preschool audience, Fred didn't shy away from difficult themes. War, divorce, racial discrimination, and grief were among the challenging topics he explored. With his signature style, Fred acknowledged the anxiety that children felt when they heard scary news stories. His reminder to "look for the helpers," advice that his mother had given him when he was a child, still resonates during times of national tragedy.

During his career Fred was celebrated for his pioneering work in children's television. In 1997, he was awarded a Lifetime Achievement Emmy Award. In 1999, he was inducted into the Television Hall of Fame. In 2002, a year before Fred's death, President George W. Bush presented Fred with the Presidential Medal of Freedom, the nation's highest civilian honor.

And Fred's legacy continues today. In 2012, PBS began broadcasting an animated series called *Daniel Tiger's Neighborhood*. Four-year-old Daniel is the son of Daniel Striped Tiger, the classic puppet from the original series. With a nod to Mister Rogers, Daniel wears a red sweater and speaks directly to his viewers, enabling a new generation of children to experience social and emotional learning through music and make-believe.

In 2018, celebrations for the fiftieth anniversary of *Mister Rogers' Neighborhood* included a commemorative US postage stamp featuring Mister Rogers and King Friday XIII—the puppet who ruled the Neighborhood of Make-Believe—and the release of an acclaimed documentary about Mister Rogers called *Won't You Be My Neighbor?*

When Fred Rogers died in 2003, America mourned its favorite neighbor—but his compassionate spirit lives on. There was no one in the world like Mister Rogers. Without a doubt he was special.

> *"What a difference one person can make*
> *in the life of another."*
> —Fred Rogers